Dad's Day Off

By Charles Perry, Jr.
Illustrations By Terencio Lopes

"Cough, Cough." Liam hears Dad coughing. Liam asked, "Dad are you okay?" Dad responds, "No Liam I am very sick. I will not be able to go to work today. You will have to make the hat deliveries on your own. There will be 6 deliveries today."
Liam says, "No problem I can make all the deliveries."

Liam was only a teenager, so he had to make his deliveries on his bicycle. Dad placed a delivery basket on Liam's bike, so when the store was busy Liam could make deliveries on his own.

PUPPA'S
PIZZA

Liam arrived at the store and placed all the hats on the counter.

B
HAT STORE
THE
HAT
STORE

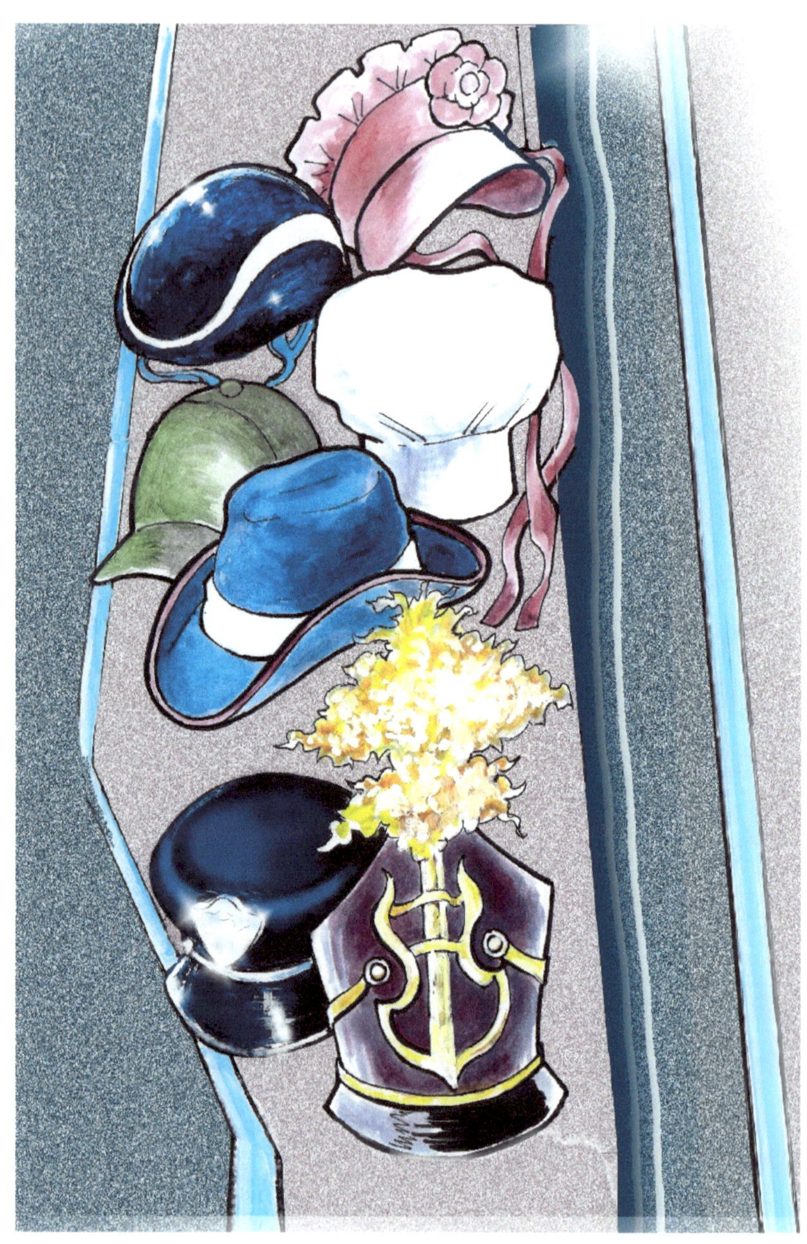

He needed to be careful
and place all the hats in
delivery boxes.

Liam's list
1. Brittney
2.Puppa's Pizza
3. Emma
4. May
5. Ms. Pat's
6. Off. Perry

The first order was a cowboy hat for Brittney. Liam liked her hat and tried it on.

Brittney

He started down the road and arrived at the ranch where Brittney worked. Liam rang his delivery bell as he arrived at the door. Brittney came walking out and smiled, "My hat has arrived." She tried it on and said, "It fits perfectly".

Liam returned to the store to pick up some more deliveries. The next stop was "Puppa's Pizza Place". This was one of his favorite places to eat.

Puppa's
Pizza place

He had a white Chef's hat for Puppa. He arrived at the pizza shop. "Hi, Puppa I have your hat." Puppa said, "Liam thank you. I was getting ready to open the doors for my delicious pizzas".

"Well, Puppa I have more deliveries I will talk to you later".

PUPPA'S
PIZZA

Looking at his deliveries
he noticed he has 2 hats
going to the same place.
He had a baseball hat for
May. He also had a
marching band hat for
Emma. They both were at
the high school practicing.
May played softball for
the Middle School and
Emma was waiting on the
football field for her
marching hat.

May
Emma

Emma spotted Liam on his bike and she shouted, "Liam, Liam I'm over here." Liam handed Emma her hat and she ran off saying "Thank you, Liam, see you at Puppa's Pizza after practice."

May was close by sitting on the bleachers with her mom. Liam very politely said, "Hi May I have your new hat for your softball game." May smiled and said, "It's time to play ball." Liam responded, "Go get 'em May."

Liam noticed the time and noticed he was behind on his deliveries. Liam decided to take a shortcut and ride his bike down the hillside behind his Dad's store. He raced down so fast that he hit a big rock on the path. The bump caused Liam's bicycle tire to go flat. Liam walked the bike to the front of the store. He was upset because he had two more deliveries.

Liam's friend, Joe was skate boarding by and said, "What's wrong Liam?" Liam sadly said, "I have two more deliveries and I only have time to make one." Joe smiled, "I can make a delivery for you on my roller skates." Liam smiled from ear to ear and said, "Thank you, Joe."

BAN

Joe took the policeman's
hat for Officer Perry.

Puppa's
Pizza
PARKING

Liam took Ms. Pat's hat
which was a fancy bonnet.
Liam told Joe to meet me
at my house after you
make the delivery.

Ms. Pat's

Boutique

Joe raced down the street and went directly into the police station parking lot.

"Off. Perry, I have your hat." Off. Perry said, "Thank you, Joe. I expected Liam to drop it off." Joe responded, "I am helping him with his deliveries."

36

Liam and Joe arrived at Liam's house at the same time to tell Liam's Dad they made all the deliveries.

His Dad was so happy. He embraced the boys and said, "Job well done. Pizza is on me today." Liam looked at his Dad and Joe and "Teamwork at it's best."

PUPPA'S
PIZZA

They all went over to
Puppa's Pizza Place to end
the day.

The End

MENU
MENU

This story was inspired by my 2 buddies, Liam & Joe. They inspire me every day just by the things they do on my school bus. I anticipate the smiles on their faces as they prepare to go to school. They both have great support from their families and friends. These boys have taught me a lot. I am a supporter of Autism, because of these 2 boys. I am blessed to have them in my life. Last but surely not least, the boys have a monitor named Brittney and I am proud to say she is the best. I am truly

grateful that Tremblay's Bus
Company assigned me to this
bus route because I would
have never met Liam & Joe
and their wonderful families.